BURNING SEASON

Yvonne Reddick is an award-winning writer, editor, ecopoetry scholar and climber. She has received a Leadership Fellowship from the Arts and Humanities Research Council, the Poetry Society's inaugural Peggy Poole Award, a Northern Writer's Award and a Creative Futures Literary Award. Her work has appeared in *The Guardian Review*, *The Poetry Review* and *The New Statesman*, and has been broadcast on BBC Radio 3 and BBC *North West Tonight*. She has published four pamphlets, including *Translating Mountains* (Seren, 2017), winner of the *Mslexia* Women's Pamphlet Competition, and *Spikenard* (Laureate's Choice, 2019), which was a poetry recommendation for early 2019 in the *London Review of Books*. Her first book-length collection, *Burning Season*, was published by Bloodaxe in 2023. Her other publications include *Ted Hughes: Environmentalist and Ecopoet* and *Magma: The Anthropocene Issue* (as editor), which was met with the BBC news headline 'Poets print climate change poetry on recycled paper with vegetable oil ink.' She is also a book critic for the *Times Literary Supplement*.

Yvonne Reddick's research has revealed that Ted Hughes lobbied politicians about pollution and that Seamus Heaney sold poems to raise funds for bog conservation. She has published climate change poetry by former oil geologists, and run nature writing workshops for organisations from Warwick Book Festival to the Ramblers.

YVONNE REDDICK

Burning Season

BLOODAXE BOOKS

ISBN: 978 1 78037 645 5

First published 2023 by
Bloodaxe Books Ltd,
Eastburn,
South Park,
Hexham,
Northumberland NE46 1BS

www.bloodaxebooks.com
For further information about Bloodaxe titles
please visit our website and join our mailing list
or write to the above address for a catalogue.

Supported using public funding by
ARTS COUNCIL
ENGLAND

Cover design: Neil Astley & Pamela Robertson-Pearce.

Printed in Great Britain by Bell & Bain Limited, Glasgow, Scotland, on
acid-free paper sourced from mills with FSC chain of custody certification.

In memory of Christopher Reddick

CONTENTS

Muirburn

My father weighed a little less than at birth.
I carried him in both hands to the pines
as October brought the burning season.
When I unscrewed the urn, bone-chaff and grit
streamed out. The smell of gunpowder.
I remembered the sulphur hiss of the match –
how he taught me to breathe on the steeple of logs
until the kindling caught and flames quickened.

That night, in sleep, I saw the forest clearing
by the moor's edge, and the ring of his ashes.
A skirl of smoke began to rise –
bracken curling, a fume of blaeberry leaves.
Ants broke their ranks, scattering, fleeing,
and a moth spun ahead of the fire-wind.
I took the path over the heath at a run.

A voice at my shoulder said, 'You'll inherit fire.'
And through the smoke I glimpsed a line of figures
on the hillside, beating and beating the heather
as the fire-front roared towards them.
A volley of shouts: 'Keep the wind at your back!'
My grandmother threshing with a fire-broom,
Dad hacking a firebreak. My stillborn brother, now grown,
sprinting for the hollow where the spring once flowed,
the whole hill flaring in the updraft.

And there: a girl, running for the riverside –
she wore my face, the shade of ash.

The Flower that Breaks Rocks

He introduced his daughters to Ben Nevis.
'You take the bearing. Line up the arrow,'

pointing to Moonlight Gully Buttress,
Minus One Gully. We didn't care

until Dad found us a saxifrage. Its blooms
were spokes of the North Star.

'*Saxifraga* means *rock-breaker.*'
Nivalis: snow-saxifrage.

Dainty Alpinist, chinking her roots into fissures
and fractures, like crampons in toeholds.

But I see now what he could only glimpse.
That she and the other Alpines – roseroots

and pearlworts – are scrambling skywards
until all that remains for them is cloud.

In Oils

1

I was nine, when my father made me leave –
he drilled an emirate with straight-ruled borders.
The heat on the runway like the breath of a foundry.
My Narnia books arrived after their voyage
along the Suez Canal, in the sea-freight.
Wearing shorts was forbidden – even for men.

Mirage city, under the warp-shimmer of fifty degrees.
Sun-beaten metal. Lightstruck glass,
the bombed-out bridge to Bubiyan Island.
At the sandstone hill on the edge of Iraq,
herdsmen turned camels loose to trigger landmines.

At school, they preached that oil was fossil light:
one barrelful did twelve years' human work.
Dad's friends talked Bonny Light, Brent Blend,
Sour Heavy Crude, counting days in gallons.
Oil was refined, but its temper had a flashpoint –

2

Fragments of Kuwait resurface. Shots, voices on the TV, half-remembered
images, hushed discussions after my light was turned out.

NAYIRAH
Only ash and rubble was left.
My sister with my five-day old nephew travelled across the desert.
No milk for the baby.

KUWAITI STUDENT
My head was bleeding. I crawled over to Samir,
trying to revive him.

13

I thought he had been pretending, like me.
Then I saw the bullet hole in his head.

ARCHIVAL FOOTAGE
Wellheads, fire-trenches, the sea alight. Planes and satellites watching
smoke-trails.

CANADIAN FIREFIGHTER
Midday, but when you could see the sky,
it didn't last.
I told them, there's no words
to describe what you're fixed to go into.

KUWAITI OIL ENGINEER
The burning oil-well howled –
sounded like a plane engine.
The Canadians capped the pipes,
then we put in new blowout preventers.
Six billion barrels of light, sweet crude.

ARCHIVAL FOOTAGE
Birds wading in the slick-ponds, a hoopoe drinking petroleum. The oiled
eagle panting for water.

IRAQI REPORTER
They used to call this the City of Peace.
(The first bombs fell at two-thirty.)
Baghdad was a ghost town in the morning,
no electricity or running water.

ARCHIVAL STILLS
Airstrike on the Basra road – the man clawed at the windscreen, trying
to smash free before the petrol tank blew. The camera blinked at his
burnt-out sockets.

It's seared into my memory, he was fighting
to save his life till he was completely burned up.

3

Between fjords and the Firth, the rig whirred
from its crown-block to the pit of its stress-cage –
my father left at dawn to work the offshore fields.
He grafted with roughnecks and a crude-talking toolpusher:
their toil slaked fuel lines, lit flarestacks, stoked motors.
Farther north, the trickle and tick of ice floes.

That year's gales uprooted dunes, hurled gulls
along Union Street; the derrick braced its anchors,
strained against the storm-surge.
                                        His chair sat empty.
The desk paperweight: a drop of Brent crude
globed in glass, the tarry slick levelling when I tilted it.
I tried to pray for breezes to ferry him home,
but all I could invoke were fields of North Sea oil:
Magnus, Beatrice, Loyal.

4

From Anchorage, Calgary, Houston or Galveston
Dad returned, jet-lagged and running fumes,
to plant English lavender on Texan time.
I'd see him at the sink, scrubbing his hands:
'I've fixed the engine!' He'd show his palms –
I watched him scouring skin that wouldn't come clean.
His shirts would smell of earth and gasoline.

* * *

He set off to go hiking, as he had a hundred and sixty-six times before (he made a note of every hill). But when night came, Dad still had not returned. The ridge of the Grey Corries: Hill of the Fawn's Valley, the Castle, Peak of the Brawling Corrie.

We rang the police, who rang Mountain Rescue. They didn't set off until the following morning. (Walkers often get lost and show up in time for breakfast.)

It was his car that they spotted first, without him in it. Then his backpack, just upstream of the waterfall.

John from Mountain Rescue wept as he drove us to the pool near the rapids. They found Dad lying face down.

Cold shock, a fall, the heart. No one knows exactly what happened. And I can't write any more. Don't ask me to write more.

Esther in the Asylum Garden

> I walked with Valerie a while, down the familiar labyrinth of shovelled
> asylum paths
>
> SYLVIA PLATH: *The Bell Jar*

To be born twice, clamber to the fig tree's summit. Swaying
in the branch-sea, you'll realise how snappable the neck's stem is,
but you won't slip, Esther. The Carmelite sister and the rabbi
– you know the yarn? Imagine this tree was theirs. She'd
pry orbs of ripeness from the twigs; he'd raise them to his lips.

Moss-carders, carpenters, miner bees: the females labour to quicken
hipless roses, whir to their nunnish cells at sundown. They outwit
aerial nets and kill-jars. But the fig's unseen flower teems with wasps.
A skep of stings. Queens enter the unripe ovary, tear
their wedding-veil wings; the tree pairs them with its prisoned males.

Tell me, whose mind isn't a fizzing hive of venom? I'm sick
of freezing baths, Doc Quinn droning on about Freud, Dad, death.
The wallpaper in these rooms is a migraine, but I'm glad you're here –
remember wading through *Finnegans Wake*, then bourbon with Yalies?
Here, they'll treat me with shocks of Metrazol or insulin.

Salvia once salved wounds; feverfew was a febrifuge. Listen: the loon's
tremolo, *cheer-up cheerily* of robins. The fig tree endures
lightning that blitzes through its crown. Come fall, the fruit will wink,
wine-purple with knowledge. Pick one that splits, and you'll bite hearts.
A globed one for Lyon, Ravenna, El Arabí: countries close as health.

That bracelet of bruised fingermarks on your wrist has healed;
you've survived entrées laced with poison, those forty
barbiturates you swallowed. Your line will live beyond the final page.
We'll climb the espalier, drive all night to Elm Street, begin
the rite to plant our second spring – come now with me.

The Gift

I wanted to write *Speak*, but it wrote *Spark*.
Loaded with cartridges, it rested on the desk.
No one dropped it or chewed the tip
but its tactics grew underhand. I tried to write

Je suis Européenne. It spoke for itself. *Je suis Iranienne*.
I unscrewed nib from body. Inside, a pipeline of what
stirred in the Cretaceous, freighted and volatile. Oceans,
continents shifted. The drillbit woke it to burn, liquid

to solid carbon-black, changing state back to ink.
Indelible blots: my hands smudged shirts, doors, tables.
Each murky fingermark printed a tiny globe,
fuel-lines from Persian Gulf to Gulf of Mexico.

A newspaper flapped to the doormat: slicked gull's
wings. EVERYTHING WRITTEN IN FIRE AND OIL.
I tried to sketch a cottage, so the gift drew smoking
rubble. A blazing refinery spoke to my line
Thank you for this beautiful Waterman pen.

Split by tyres and buried in leaf-mulch, some lose their seed-coats and turn tannic red. The fuses of roots. Even broken, their furious will to unfurl.

The acorns spring up in autumn. A green winter, frostless.

I gather two handfuls and put them in a Tupperware box, in damp tissue, like my childhood – the sunflower in the jam jar. The roots thirst for groundwater. They live on my writing desk, watered every weekday, neglected and parched at weekends when I'm in the Peaks. An anxious mother of seedlings.

Flower and gall. Lamp black or oak-apples for ink. That's what I tell myself the planting season will bring.

Fire-seed

Saplings in neck braces: infant willow, oak fledging
into leaf. Their roots have hit the quarry's midden.

You hawthorn, the delicate cling of your spines.
Little Northerners, you'll keep
your first winter close in a dark band.

But hornbeams will outlive six kingdoms and weather
sixty governments. A yew can remember Domesday.

The land's hollowed edge.
You trees are the only children I can bear
to watch growing tall.

More firework than flower-spike,
buds brazen in hottest pink

on the torched slope, where ferns were coal
fossils, and the heather's
remains scribbled lampblack

on my ankles. Sprouting
from blitzed rubble
the flighted seeds an old man's ear-hair –

the effrontery of rosebay,
its refusal to lie buried.

Birches break through: all their intrusive thoughts.
Autumn unleashes their million offspring. They clamber
the excavated sandstone; wanting the spoil-
heaps, they'll conquer them by force of numbers.

The whole heath gossips to itself, stirring
root-synapses. All that telepathy under your feet.
A mill-town's junkyard, this moor; heaps of torqued
wire lying low under scrub and heather. It's not
as if anyone wants this land, apart from the birches.

I've been instructed to uproot their scrubby
empire. Our conservation brief implies words like
extirpate and *birch-hunt*. Apparently, no one else
feels that their fey trunks evoke Rivendell
(besides, glades like these are haunted by returnees
home from the farthest woods.) Obedient,
I clamp each wrist-thick trunk between the haft
and foot of the uprooter, and heave. The network
creaks and ruptures; I rip up moss and bilberry.

A mature tree will nurse its neighbour's
stump. That sprout rises from a mouldering log;
its parents fairy-ringed with waxcaps and boletus.
Beneath ground, a red stem linking stand to grove,
the line between two charges of explosive green.
The heath can't contain its birches,
swarming over the town's borders and beds.

Trees find me at work, breathing from the bookleaves.
Their winglets blow through my office window, as if
birches could root in concrete, and elbow through
a carpet. The seeds infiltrate my books, sift
and lodge between *Slow Violence* and *The Silver Bough*.

The Frontier of Water

His afterlife starts in monochrome. The body is two-thirds
fluid, so I baptise him in sulphates, bathe his image in acid;
dredge up my father's grin in a room that shutters out light.

The snapshot emerges; he taught three of us to skip stones
across a torrent-pool, its bank stippled with footprints.
A splash trapped in mid-air. In the next frame, he stands
where the watershed unfurls in thirty braided
falls: la Fontaine d'or, la Cascade de Lyre.
He said dams would breach, but boulders endure
until the flood braces its shoulder to granite.

A sting of saltwater blurs the edge of sight;
the negatives bring absence into focus. *Learn to tread
water*, he'd say. *The flood musters; everything is fluent.*

*

Thirty fathoms under the lake lies the frontier.
He sculled our boat over mussel-shells, shells
of mortars, drowned hulls; a silhouette caught *contre jour*.
The years trickle past in the darkroom that registers
his hair as a blaze and sun on Mont Blanc in noir.

Eye drawn to altitude, he captured the rubbled glacier.
Streams weeping from Mont Dolent, Mont Maudit, milder
Mont Tendre. The cold unlatched its crypt of crevasses:
a man found his father, young as him, beneath an iceshelf.
Two mountaineers caught Polaroids of a tattooed warrior
rising from the Ice Age, stained with three murders.

That morning Dad stumbled at the high pass;
he laughed, but the hand I gripped was cold and bloodless.

*

The next shot sees me finding a four-leaf clover –
I snapped the stem, pressed it between the covers
of his battered guidebook, *La haute route alpine*.
Beneath the flyleaf, three leaves remain.

He taught me tactics for developing the positives:
masks for contours, shadow smoking from a burn.
I still treasure his album of small lives.
His line links me to sepia girls on the beach at Léman,
unsmiling violinists who crossed the Rhine;
each age-flecked print bears a version of his face.

My screen flickers with a gorge, the dammed
pool trapping birches, sky, heathery foreland;
three figures at the water-mirror, willing him to surface.

Madness Lake

Not even when we scaled
the ice-scoured Dalle
did I think it was possible

that he, like a glacier, could change state
from solid to intangible
in the pause between my heartbeats.

Grinning and mopping his sunburnt brow,
my father seemed imperishable
as the snow-hooded Pointe overhead.

When we reached the lake
the glacier calved with a gunshot,
jostled its floating bergs –

its snout already retreating.
Twenty years to the day
since we last trekked this crisscross path

to Lac de Folly: Madness Lake.
The sign still reads 'Caution: year-round snow'
but the floes are meltwater –

my grief now ten months deep.

Fired Earth

MAN SURVIVES BUSHFIRE HIDING IN POTTERY KILN

CNN

'Total explosion of everything in the garden –
tree canopies in flame as the fire crowned,'
but this is the potter's garden. He knows
the candlebarks and eucalyptus crave heat

to split the vessels that cup their seeds,
that their children take root after fire.
'The light was this metallic, luminous glow,'
so as the road caught, he shut himself
in what he calls a 'coffin-kiln'.

Single-stone porcelain, ironstone from shale,
opal cinder bowls, vases spun from river-clay,
blackware glazed by the volcano's basalt –
they cracked and charred in the workshop.

But he can transfigure cow bones and fruit-tree ash
into tea bowls and refectory dishes.
'I drank my water bottle dry. I was shit scared,'
he said, as anyone would be.

The pot-store, the vegetable patch,
roads, hills and trees, burnt white.
He crawled from the kiln. Wiping the soot
from his eyes, he saw his house, still standing.

Superb Lyrebird

I snatch the songs right out of their throats – throw
copied hoots at sleepy owls, squall and chortle

in concert with kookaburras, fooling the flock. Look,
I parrot the jackhammer, beatbox the *chap-tock-tack* of nails,

splice whipbird cries with workmen's whistling, take the piss
out of those hard-hatted wingless fleawits: *Nice job, no sunblock.*

Voicebox, toolbox, I rifle both; mash up folksong with song-thrush.
Call me mimic, supreme fibber. (What's the lyricist if not a liar,

or a lyric but a mix-tape of thrown voices?)
I can call in chainsaw, car alarm, fire alarm, fire.

Yesterday, the song dried in my throat in the forest.
Charcoal pillars. Mute ash. Ash hush.

December

Mould smothers the acorns in its dirty fleece. I've let them rot.

The thinnest snow. It melts as it touches car bonnets, roofs, salty pavements.

A winter so warm that my tomato plant remains green under the glass roof, flecked with mildew.

Stay at home.

I take trowelfuls of compost and bury their frail roots and mouldering bodies. Still, one of them has the beginnings of a shoot. If it grows, it will spend the first years of its life pot-bound.

At the Corrie of the Birds

Two figures emerged from lightless spruces,
one wrapped a delicate arm around the other.
They scanned a map of densely-contoured crags
for a chance that was becoming remote.

Just visible, the walkers scoured
the feet of Caisteal's rock-fortress,
combed the heather that fledges the base
of its escarpment. A pair of crows, circling.

Not a bootprint on the hill between streams.
A rock at the falls' lip rolled, poised –
cracked with the noise a limb makes, on impact.

Two in the morning, I jolted awake.
My mother crept across the floor above.
I rushed upstairs to hold her hand.

Wet dawn surfaced at the window
like a drowned face still fixed in a smile.
The sergeant creaked up our staircase,
to tell us –
                        an animal cry
broke from my lungs.

The asphodels in late bloom.
At the dam, a bloated lamb
floated with its escort of flies.

One figure yelled from the ravine's brink
as a mother hawk calls for a nestling
that opened its wings
and fell.

On the Alaskan Peak We Never Climbed

My father dodged a rumbling boulder
of splintering granite:
'Tuck your head in!' to me below,
'Hang on!' my left fingers scrabbling at holds,

right hand struggling to place a cam
as the groaning rockfall
dimmed the sun overhead.
Earth shuddered to a standstill

and I hauled myself to join him
on the cropped grass of the col,
hand quaking in his.
There, to the west, his next mountain –

its horseneck ridge crested with pines,
head in a cowl of storm.
His hair had grown
from grizzled to deep brown

and death had washed him of fear
in the mapless land we tracked in my sleep.
A path wound
westward, through barbed spruces –

he walked ahead, carrying the compass
that still hangs on my wall,
turned back to beckon me
along the path I could not follow.

* * *

Loyal, Munro, Schiehallion: subsea fields named for Scotland's most stunning peaks. Schiehallion was my father's favourite mountain.

There is poetic licence in the naming of oilfields. Galahad, North Valiant and Ivanhoe speak of the namers' pretensions to chivalry. Others are christened for executives' wives and children (Dad worked with an oil reservoir called Beatrice). There is a Golden Eagle oilfield; another is called Ekofisk, although the 'echo fish' is imaginary. Someone with a nose for a fine single malt called an oilfield Glenlivet.

Ravenspurn and Newsham were baptised for villages swallowed by the (rising) North Sea.

Storm Petrel

ABERDEEN
He departed to raise the Jurassic.
The hill-wind on my father's face, before weeks
aboard the rig. North of the peak
where the road would end, he spent Sunday
trudging to the Nevis cairn.

The pilot made him walk a line.
'Drysuit? Lifejacket?'
– 'Check.'
'Reddick?'
– 'Ready!'
He watched the cities shrinking:
Stonehaven, Peterhead,
Aberdeenshire's rain-grey granites.

Over the waves, the blade of Shetland.
They named the oil-platforms
for birds: Merlin, Osprey, Brent.
Touchdown offshore
for the two-week static voyage.

STORM PETREL, CAPE VERDE COAST
So seabound, she stumbled on land –
tough light approaching, though
days were no longer.
Dust hazing the air, dust
in the petrel's throat and feathers;
sand clouding the sea where she dived.
By the rock-caves, fishermen with their catch
of conches sat on hot stones,
cracking the chambers of shells.

The Sahara had flown to sea
on the Harmattan –
the conch-fishers scarved
their eyes to watch the petrels
patter wings and feet on waves,
stepping north on water.

DUNLIN A PLATFORM
The rig-lights fiery on choppy breakers.
In his bunk, sardine-canned
with four dorm-mates,
my father lay restive under a thin blanket.

Noise jackhammered everyone's eardrums –
drilled through cabins,
girders. Dad felt the weather turn.
The men perched

over an ocean above
a deeper ocean of sweet, black oil.
The rig boomed like a petrol tanker,
its hull pitching over the North Atlantic.

Dinner was mock chop, double chips and peas,
then double chips and peas with mock chop again.
Failure to hold the handrail
was a sackable offence.
My father learnt how
to say *No sé hablar español*
at night classes. Workers on
an iron-and-concrete outcrop
need instructive hobbies. They miss
their women, their families, grow fractious –

STORM PETREL, NORTH ATLANTIC
Scavenging flotsam:
shrimps, krill, moon jellyfish,
those translucent creatures
called *by-the-wind sailors*.

Petrels can smell oil a mile off,
will scrounge whale blubber
or scraps from a salmon farm.

They follow in the wake of trawlers.

DUNLIN A PLATFORM
A favourite pastime is birding. Blown off course,
birds are enticed by rig-lights. They know
these angular sea-rocks
gather rainwater. 'One morning,'
my father said, 'an osprey,
right up there on the crown block.'

Other émigrés: fieldfares, bramblings,
the injured short-eared owl that flew
landward in the helicopter with the drilling crew.

A seal that surfaced and offered a sardine
to the scaffolder on the abseil line –
they locked gazes, eyes round as portholes.

The best was the corncrake
rasping by the draw-works –
all hundred and two men
raised their glasses of Kaliber.

STORM PETREL, NORTH ATLANTIC

The petrel was heading for Mousa,
that crumb of rock holding
her nest in the prehistoric cairn.
She and her mate would tend
a quartz-white egg,
each parent brooding the warm, live pebble,
before the weather turned and they
returned to the Cape Verde winter.

DUNLIN A PLATFORM

Wind woke and filled its lungs.
Three-metre waves slammed the legs
of Dunlin A. The flame blown backwards
down the steel throat of the flarestack dragon.
Whiplash rain, near-horizontal.
A crackle on the intercom:
Deck's slippery, boys!

No one slept that night: the storm bawled
through chinks in cabins, and rain
battered its fists on the roof. The rig
an ocean liner, tethered but foundering.

Bloodshot sky that morning; the blown gale sullen.
The men went on deck to hand-line for mackerel.
My father told me, with a catch
in his throat, of the disgorger,
the gaff, their dulling eyes.
A gift of slick-blue bodies for my mother
when he returned, the red
wound in each hulled belly.

STORM PETREL, DUNLIN A PLATFORM

At the first whiff of fish-guts
they arrived like a squall:
the flock treading water
to the rig with its sea-legs.

One of them crash-landed by the galley.
Draggled feathers; only her head moved,
flicking right and left in panic.
The rig cook, once a ship's chef,
offered leftover cod.
'It's a petrel. Never seen them so early.
Sailors say they bring heavy weather.'

My father cradled the exhausted traveller,
lighter than the balsa glider he assembled
as a boy. He ran his fingers
along the wire-like struts of wing-bones,
checked the ruddering tail, the submarine keel-bone
and launched the storm-petrel
into an unsettled sky.

January

The hardest freeze since the wind arrived from the steppes.

The city hibernates. On Hartshead Pike, grass has hardened to porcupine quills. Blackstone Edge is treeless, with a clear line of white. A rowan I planted four winters ago on the moor is half-smothered in a drift. The quiet of snow, when all you can hear is the creak of your footprints.

I hope that the acorns are dormant, but can't tell.

Coal Measures

Veins

My father's origin-myths and Genesis: Silurian, Permian, Carboniferous.
'Take this chunk of coal,' he said, by the grate's searing mouth. 'You're
holding solid light, millennia old.'

Way back, the father of the finger was a fin.
In that distant swamp forest, the eye
was compound. Whirring the air of the fen,

a six-winged mayfly; its faceted sight
sharp for devil-frogs launching into wetland
pools, the air quartered by drone-huge dragonflies.

If you could descend into strata, their underground
storeys, you'd come face to face with a salamander
heavy as a caiman, hauling herself landward

from depths to shallows, to her breathing egg under
bank-side fronds. Chlorophyll the only colour,
drinking sunshine in a riot of verdure.

Uncurling tree-ferns, horsetail, clubmosses,
their rise, seeding, and death in graves of peat –
leaf-layer on layer, their branch-tangle masses

crushed by the water-tonnage, rock-weight.
Fool's gold winked between fissures.
The coal in hibernation, hoarding occult sunlight.

Black Callerton

My grandmother: 'Robert had no children,' a smoke-wreath scrolling
from her Silk Cut, 'but he had a brother. George had loads of relatives.
Both my parents were Stephensons – my name before I married.
My father distilled oil from coal.'
   Mum heard her in-laws' Stephenson stories every Christmas,
for thirty-five years.

They entered earth and the underground forest
of stone stems. George and son
winched on a windlass a thousand feet down,
the lad's fingers gripping the wicker basket.

Their eye-pupils gaped, then calibrated
to the lamps' wavering. The mainway
flanked with shafts, wide as railway
tunnels, channelled and galleried.

Father and boy waded through muddy slurries
to a side-cave, which limbed and branched
like a lung-tube, into smaller shafts,
each with its air-vents, its honeycomb pillars.

George: 'I worked here as a lad: brakesman,
then enginewright. Taught myself to fettle lamps.'
Breathing coaldust, the reek of firedamp –
grit in Robert's eyes. The dense air leaden.

The hewers, picks smashing at lignite,
raised their stone god from the rockface, sweating.
George patted the seam, its deep-night glisten:
'My engines Black Diamond and Hope ignite

coal for firepower. We brighten Great Britain.'
'Father, can I turn steam into horsepower?'
A boy Robert's age crawled through rust-water
towards the spoil-heap, with his stone-cart burden.

Rocket

Twenty revolutions per minute, industry
gaining momentum. A moment of pivots,
coke-fired furnaces.
      Extinguished dragon
with corroded steam-valves, twisted boiler-tube
intestines. My father would have covered miles to see
you, stand on the stoker's step and release
the steam-valve's voice, bringing his burnt-
offering of coal.
   Your chimney's quenched,
those absurd wooden wheels are soot-grimed,
your broken nameplate wears its copperplate
patina. But your carbon-black smoke still
sears the sky, high and distant.
      Stepping from the platform
to Euston Square, I came face-to-face with
a far-off relative – young Stephenson in stovepipe
hat and bronze-cast sideburns, lording it over
London plane trees in his frock-coat.
One of my father's folk, but no more like me
than beetle-browed Darwin. The city's
acid drizzle corroding his hawk-nose and jaw.

Revenant

The many forms he will outwear: leaf, shell, limestone.

He flies
from the smokestack, soars into weather.
Wind buffets his particles in clouds.
The sun glares. My Prospero-father, stirring storms in the atmosphere.

A mote of him drifts over the North
Sea he once drilled. He feeds the churn of wavecrests, their spill and furl.

Drowned god,
my father sinks in the ocean.
Algae – speck-sized coracles – transform
him to fuel.
They will be laid to rest on the sea-bed.

The ocean deepens. He drifts to the sea-floor, touches
brine with an acid taint. Coral bones dissolve as he
passes.
(He took me to gather sand-dollars, mermaids' purses, strandline leavings.)

A molecule brushes an oakleaf.
The tree inhales him, splicing him with sunshine.
(My father's pride in his Scots Pine, evergreen in its garden urn.)

No matter
is destroyed.
That speck of him enfolded by reeds, swallowed by the shallows, will crystallise –
a bright-black vein
of coal.

* * *

I watch the city through it – contact lenses are oil in the eyes. It's in the keyboard on my desk, the fibres of my dress.

The plastic cup leaches it into my arteries. An essential ingredient in credit cards and antidepressants.

It bubbles up from the tarmac outside.

*

'It was an era,' said my mother, 'and like coal, it's coming to an end.'

Frankincense

My mother sounded Earth's deep architecture,
listening for the fossil ocean's echo.

(This was five years before the ultrasound
showed me on a grainy screen in Glasgow.)

She saw the thirsty shrub by a dry well
in a desert burnt white, the salt city's hinterland.

Oilfields reek of tar, but Omani frankincense
is the world's most fragrant: a scent that suggests

the Magi, trekking the desert from Persia
to offer the tree's tears to a small god.

'Women in Salalah use it to perfume their linen,'
she told me. 'But it looked like a gorse bush,

you know, the ones you see here on the Common.
Its twigs were barren, as if burnt.

In winter, leaves break from the stems
and flowers unfurl.'

Cristaux de Roche

Their gleam haunts my sleep:
the rocks and ores
from my grandmother's trove
in her loft at Lausanne.

When she heard that the clast
in her breast was cancer,
she willed them to me –
they lie dormant
in the box under my bed.

Relics of her grandfather Resteau,
the one with the alpenstock
and geologist's hammer.
My thoughts trail him

up Monts to the cusps
of Spitzen and Corni,
as I touch the points
of clustered quartz, a tiny massif.

Our forebear's dip-pen copperplate
names *sphène* and *galène*,
his labels mapping each to its origins.

We're family, but a man
of his Victorian inkhornisms
would be *vous* to me,
the accented stranger
who picks through his dusty specimens.

Nights, they take root in bedrock:
I see them grow to towering altitudes
of névé and depth-hoar.

Waking, I polish the facets
of a feldspar spire,
cup its lucent Matterhorn
in my palms.

Translating Mountains from the Gaelic

A pebble on the tongue
and a chockstone in the throat:

Beinn Laoghail becomes Ben Loyal,
Beinn Uais eroded to Ben Wyvis,

Bod an Deamhain
turns from Demon's Penis to Devil's Point,

my voice a stream-gorge
where quartz chunks clatter.

Last summer, I shouldered my red rucksack,
a water-flask, and a vial of his ash.

A deerfly, its eyes peridot ringstones
hovered to steal my blood,
my language a trespasser.

I poured my father's English dust
to feed the roots of the hill's oldest pine.

Let the rain seep through him,
Schiehallion transforming him to earth.

Shadowtime

a huge clock...designed to tick for 10,000 years

THE LONG NOW FOUNDATION.

Under the mountain, it ticks once a year
in a cavern deep as the massif is tall.

Start the climb through the desert at dawn.
There's no water; you must ascend two thousand feet.

The clock's gears creak. Last time it pealed its stroke,
the ice-shelf groaned, calved into the sound.

The door is steel-rimmed jade. Turn the handle;
step inside. It thuds shut in earth-core darkness.

You can make out a mineshaft, deep as a cathedral.
Above, the faintest blink of light.

You must clamber to the summit now,
up a spiral staircase, through the guts of rock.

There's the thousand-pound counterweight
hanging like a stone whale's heart.

Not the sort of time that flickers in a wristwatch.
This is the span of ice ages, civilisations.

Wind it – the strike of cliff-sized bells.
The clock knows the mountain under you

is moving. A dome of sapphire glass: the dial
shows the thousand-year walk of unfixed stars.

This clock can strike the time through nuclear strikes.
This clock will tick until the sea arrives.

Of the Flesh

I still wanted to free that cry when I painted the beef carcass.
I have not yet succeeded.

CHAÏM SOUTINE

The kick of your father's gun –
the shot
sent a buck-rabbit
thrashing in convulsions –
its cry entered me.

You twisted the neck. It lay
abruptly silent. Still,
after three years, I hear the cry.

But I, too, have stripped
the skin like a robe
and slid a hand between the strakes
of ribs, to feel
the still-warm heart.

I have returned
the blank gaze of a peeled head.

But when I saw the creature's arms
thrown wide, baring the emptied chest,
its voice of wire
filled my ears.

That night, an air rifle cracked through sleep
by the sett in the woods
and the cry seized my throat –

broke off, severed
as your fingers found my nape.

Spikenard

I trailed your flint and bayleaf scent to the porch,
but someone else's perfume was mixed with yours –

coiling with jonquils, spikenard, and a tendril of musk.
I paused at your alderwood door. Like one in ivy

you were wreathed in the cologne I bought you:
Terre. Its heart-chord silex and bitter orange,

the base-note (which strikes deep roots) is Atlas cedar.
I remembered how I'd settle my cheek on your chest

to feel the stroke of your heart, until your fragrance
steeped my pores, and I'd breathe you in for weeks.

I pictured her hands at your belt, in that attic room –
my key still sprang the bolt.

Firesetter

You left me a two-word note. Lying
under our bed was your forgotten lighter.
I ran to the forest and held its flame to a fir-cone –

the resiny scales were the fuse of a Molotov cocktail.
I hurled it over your deer fence, into
the spruces where we once heard nightjars.

Three months of drought; those trees were jackstraws.
A flicker in the tinder, bird-call panic.
The easterly sighed on the flames as I walked away.

I pictured your garden: a sheaf of flaming letters
where the paper birch once stood.
The oaks, hands of bone with a furnace backdrop.

Two days in, my brushfire had swallowed fifty hectares.
Sirens through the heat-haze,
villagers were silhouettes with hose-reels.

Peat earth: fire skulked underground at a smoulder.
Wheat burned from the root up.
On the third day, a rain of soot. The school stood empty.

Nine days on, fire-crews drained the lake,
the village abandoned under a haze.
The ninth night – I found the staircase

leading to air, the bedroom blasted open,
the ribs and roof-tree smoking.
You stepped from the door's charred gape.

Kindling

She knocked one night, as the clock tricked
through shortening dark. Brows and eyes

kohl copies of mine, but her braid was auburn.
She read my face, cotched by the stove, and stirred

the embers. 'Make yourself at home,' she
told me, gorging the brazier on my best coal.

We were up with the next day to prune my apples –
Summer King, Beauty of Bath – hard frost hissed

at the heat of her instep. A fingertip tapped
on bark: nude pear trees frothed with blossom.

Mayweed and nightshade rioted across
the January field. The sky a flashover.

To teach me pyrography, she scorched her name,
two letters from mine, into the mantel;

I bit my yell in two when ('Come on, dare you!')
she turned the branding-iron on my forearm.

Joe said he'd flown to meet partners in Frankfurt;
the flags and thatch creaked themselves to sleep.

I ghost-crept to the en-suite, and caught
her in the bathtub blowing him alight

so I bolted downstairs, triple-clicked the locks,
and gave that pair and the house a gasoline shower.

These fingers are still webbed with scars,
Joe's bought a flat in Westend. My hair has grown back red.

The size of my little fingernail, but unmistakably an oak-leaf.

The ground was locked in ice last month, so I've kept them in pots under glass. The courtyard where I'm raising them is an old textile warehouse by the canal. I'm not supposed to keep them here. But no one has noticed yet.

The wind levelled a two-century ash in Worsley Woods last week.

How will I get the oaks to the edge of the forest without hurting their stems? They'll need tree guards – I've not raised them from seed to be devoured by deer.

Fossil Record

FIRST SHELL – 3LB HOWITZER

Unexploded by the fireplace,
bright brass, holding the tongs.
Emptied of cordite. Quiet.

My grandfather – if I dredge him from memory –
clipped back and sides.
Sweet peas and slug-traps
outside his shipshape house.
A naval rating's manual, foxed
with years. I'm trying to raise his voice.

Torpedo hit. The crew ran for the lifeboats.
The word 'men', for his friends. The word
'lost', for the inevitable.
His was the war for the gunmetal North Sea. I can't
for the life of me recall who gave him that Howitzer case –
his uncle, who lay low in the shell-hole?

But I do know this: the seep
from an extinct sea oiled that conflict.
'Hearing is the last to go,' my aunt said
by his hospital bed, as he drifted.
I called in the whorls of his ear, but he'd sunk deep.

SECOND SHELL – UNREFINED BRENT CRUDE SAMPLE

Monkey-board, mosquito bill, Christmas tree.

Dad learnt the jargon from his father –
nicknames for the platform's living steel.

Nodding donkey, cat-head, bull-nose.

Power. Energy. The fuel-line
pumping through veins.

Upstream, midstream, downstream.

I'd press my ear to his heart's brittle chambers,
hear the two-stroke pulse and break of valves.

Stress cage, kill line.

THIRD SHELL – REEF-BUILDING BIVALVE

I heard an ancient ocean in its hollow.
Dad brought it back
from Abu Dhabi, a sandstone place
I couldn't pronounce.

He told me it lived in the depths.
Builder of continental shelves
the size of a soup bowl,

but hollowed like a lamp, a cracked jerry-can.
Oil-trap, the wealth of Gulfport and Arabian Gulf,
a creature that plummeted off the edge of the Cretaceous.

FOURTH SHELL

The slogan: *HELL.*
Instead of the fuel company's scallop,
Dad's shirt branded with a red and yellow skull.
A parting gift.

Whitby. Would that be 1989?
The shore's shale pages, printed
by an older seabed.

Sifting fissile layers of silt-beds,
I hunted ammonites, and it found me –
'Looks like a bullet,' Dad said, 'but it's a belemnite,'
the core that once held together
fins, tentacles, underwater eyes.

I tucked it between fingers.
Thick and unwieldy
as the graphite-tipped stub
that rounded my first
laborious letters.

The North Sea leafing through sea-dulse and bottle-caps.

Ptarmigan

Even their eyelids are feathered.
The most High Arctic of British birds,
that cry like the clacking of pebbles.

Beakless and unclawed, we needed picks,
crampons, down jackets, and four pine-logs
crackling in the grate at Corrour.

In December, a scouring wind on the Devil's Point
sent us scurrying to the Rock of Tailors
(named for the five caught out in a blizzard).

New Year, and the burn is in spate.
Lady's mantle blooms, and gnats swither
from hollows between boulders.

But those Ice Age refugees require
weather from beyond the north wind,
a snow-cloak to outfox the eagles –

there they huddle in a melting drift.
Step too close, and they burst into flight,
a snowstorm towards the Angels' Peak.

Rime

Barbed wire muffled by frost,
snow snuffing light of out-of-season gorse.

Grass on the spine of Skiddaw hardens
to plumes, as if shed by swans

following the Pole Star. Snowflakes
stipple our gloves. My love picks

a heath-rush reed-stem
that has frozen to a quill pen

and on the wind, writes to spell
my name, spindrift rising from the fell.

I fear the extinction of winter.
So, in a drift, I sketch a snowshoe hare,

then snowy owls and snow-buntings,
to call up birds, blizzards in their wings.

Hare at Haslingfield

We both freeze.
You watch me with moon-wide stare.

Tawny forehead, dark-dipped ears –
I want to stroke

your fallow-coloured fur
with my numb fingers.
Your eye mirrors level horizons,

winter wheat under shifting cirrus,
a girl on a bike, stopped dead.

For a second, January thaws to March.

Your ears prick at sounds beyond my earshot.
A start: ramshackle hops

that quicken to full stretch.
I yearn to hold the five heartbeats

that it takes you to scud
to your form, scraped in chalk

among hedgerow roots.
Catch them, clasp

your silky warmth to my chest.

March

I looked out at the courtyard this morning and realised I had seven oaks.

Two have leaves familiar from my school crest. The oldest oak now has three leaves – all those solar cells. Five look more like green and red toothpicks than trees.

'What on earth are you going to do with them all?' my sister asks.

Sevenoaks, the town, has had its oaks uprooted and replaced, vandalised and replanted.

Imagines

That garden of émigrés and locals: sacred
fig, date palm. I was sent to clip the shockhead
orange tree, and dropped the shears when I saw
I'd committed murder: an inch-worm, halved.

Chubby infant pythons, its four siblings
cowered under leaves. My sister and I salvaged them,
provisioned them with lime-twig offcuts, camouflaged
from sparrows and the boys who dismembered
soldier-ants in Science.

Seven years since the swarm of Nighthawks
burst the sound-barrier, each bearing its high-
explosive clutch, zeroing on Baghdad. Shots
imaged the troops, mantis-eyed in gas-masks.

They shredded leaves to veins for a fortnight
then inverted their skins, like the werewolves
that stalked my *Grimms' Tales*. Armoured
chrysalids folded their flight.

North of the border, the local dictator unleashed
nerve-gas trialled on insects. Birds fell to earth
from nests, dogs choked on bloody foam; finally,
people hacked up their lungs. That memory still
stung behind the eyelids. When Tornados howled
overhead, their sonic boom detonated the night-
terrors of my sister.

We watched their eclosion – damp wing-rags
unscrolling like hibiscus petals, the oil-sheen
streaked with lemon. I couldn't say whether their checked
dappling was the likeness of a silk prayer-rug, or
a stained-glass icon.

Four chequered swallowtails, flexing
symmetrical wings. We watched each
dart through the doorway,
into the flowering season.

Burning Season

Six years dead, Dad rakes the old year's rags together,
the chestnut's jaundiced hands, embers of elm.
His footprints thaw the frost that hoars the grass,

but, like sparks or static, he stutters in and out of focus.
Sunlight amber as whiskey, stretched shadows.
The Bramley lit with fruit that wasps have hulled.

> An earlier October. Aberdeen. Dad called from the Emirates.
> 'Mum picked the last pear. There was ice
> on the playground.' 'It's forty-five here – I'm sunburnt.'

> Other autumns. Dad standing under the conker tree,
> the smell of mouldering leaves. I reached the trunk's lowest knot.
> Bristling husks and weighty, dark-eyed seeds.

> Hingeing years. Dad clipping oleanders.
> Date palms, first drops pocking the sand. Desert thunder
> over the glass-and-tarmac city. Geckos scurried up the kitchen wall.

> And later still. He sawed an infected limb
> of the Bramley, mistletoe creeping with white roots
> in the wood's veins, draining it. That tree still leafs.

Now he heaps twigs and mildewed apples.
On the wind, the smell of that summer
the moor caught light, mixed with mould and spores.

He pours the spirit, flicks the lighter,
cusses when the flame spits, then whistles Santana
as he works the rake around the stragglers.

The leaves are dank and mulching, slow to catch,
but as the smoke curls, woodlice start their exodus,
millipedes unscroll – dashes from a singed page,

a red admiral zigzags, the edge of a blackened letter.
'Here, chicken, help me with these logs.'
The bonfire rises to my height. Sweat beads his brow,

he seems not to notice his best shirt is smouldering
(he wore it to his funeral). 'Keep feeding it!'
I inch towards him, until its heat is on my face,

come so close I fear my cheeks will blister.
Ash in my eyes. Ash at the back of my throat.
I reach out, although it scorches, before he leaves –

I try to throw my arms around his neck.
Three times, I'm hugged by smoke.

Waterland

There are still pike in Jesus Ditch. The length of three finger-joints,
quicker than dactyls. Gone before you can say 'Jack Pickerel.'
Drowned land, drained land, where earth is silt and blood and river.
Fen Ditton stippled with pools, Milton's vocal reeds.
City built on water, don't you know the Wash is inching closer?

Everything swayed by the way
of water, both path and walker.

A drift of apples drips from a tree.
Hazelnuts flow past on the water's skin,

nutshell nacelles channelled to its brim.
Flash of a flank, the surface speaking circles.

A bargeman on the far bank plays blues from a different delta: *If it keeps
on rainin', levee's gonna break...*

George Gordon stabled his mare
in the meander meadow.
They swam naked and unsaddled, watched by yellow irises.
Along the bank, he walked
a bear.
His pool is jammed by a concrete weir.

When the levee breaks, mama, you got to move.

'More Côtes du Rhône, Amira?'
'I'll grab a beer.'
'Cassie, read my chart!'
'I'm better with cards.'

'You irrational hippies. Haven't you heard of probability theory?'
'Sssssh! She needs to concentrate.'

'You've drawn the Moon. Watch for undertows and tiderips, the lake's
skin of ice.'
'The junction by the Parade's already underwater.'

Names become water-
colour: Swavesey,
Fenstanton, Waterbeach.

Past flytips, brambles
and fields cropped by shearlings,

I swam in spring fishrise
through weed–clotted water.

The arches spoke echoes.
The current led to waterlilies –

a damselfly nymph shed its skin
on mine and dried its wings

but autumn found a drowned man
floating where I'd swum.

If I ever reach the Head of the River, I'll raise a glass to my father's
ghost – out there on the freezing Isis, his crew plying eight blades.
'Pull like you're pulling a townie off your granny!'

...what it takes to make a mountain man leave his home.

Water crowfoot city, willow-roots in your cellars. City of Daphnia, winter coughs and Weil's disease. Sloe city, jade vine city. Your fellowship of swans and muntjac.

We stopped dead at a giant bronze hare –
it stood in the garden of a dissolute peer.
My man said he wished he'd trespassed
over the boundary fence and pissed.

Ely's belfry sails on wetland mist. Eel Isle, culverts of fish-poachers and fyke-nets.
My friend Ely trapped an eel and kept her till she silvered. She was thirsty for salt – slipped her tank and slithered back to her sea-road river. Each eel an ell of Atlantic.

Goin' down. Goin' down.

Winter nights when the Granta can't
rest in its bed. Casts its coverlet across
the meadows, floats over the Orgasm
Bridge as mist, sleepwalks in the courts.

Old stream who hushed me when the horizon seemed to capsize.

When the levee breaks, mama, you got to move.

Streets of dumpster foxes and essay crises, from Cam Causeway to Mariner's Way. Town of smashed bottles, chucked bike-tyres cluttering Bin Brook.

The North Sea remembers its channels
and you, city of rivers, will need to weather it.

The skeleton whale in the Zoology Museum
back in its element. Darwin's fossil sea-
lilies stretching their stone tendrils.

Carved gryphons sprout gills and algae.
The Fellows of Bradbrook College

sit at high table in an underwater dome.
A library sails between clocktowers,
mooring where it's needed.

Old waterway, bless me in outwash,
reed-roots,
ground glass.

Set me adrift
surrounded by grave-goods:
a hairclip, china
cups. Leaves of a tea-bush
for these warming Northern latitudes.

When your willowed meanders
roll under the seabed,
a woman will pan the dredger's silt
for lithics and bone splinters.

The sediment will birth
cracked tankards, bottlecaps,
a shucked-off ring (now tarnished),
the broken urn of my pelvis.

My fragments will lie in a vitrine
in the floating museum
with coin-hoards, scabbard chapes,
the last Fenland bittern.

Mei rang – told me she was carrying
a girl. She kicks and pivots in her water-bed,
passenger voyaging towards the light.
'Tell me some strong female names –'

When the levee breaks, mama, you got to move.

My sister's children's children will
weigh anchor. Sleep over the waves,
hunt under them. Raise
fish, graze kelp, their voices remembering
gills. They'll listen
for whales in the shell of the ear.

Carina in the sky-sea, pray for us.
Capricorn of slow nights, lead us.
Vela, grant us a following wind.
Cetus of the depths, uplift us.

City setting sail, barge-and-tarpaulin town. The meadows, seagrass.
Octopus in the undercroft, barnacles on skylights. During storms, the
bells of Caius and Queen's still ring beneath the water. Your children
plotting courses for all points of the compass.

ACKNOWLEDGEMENTS

I am grateful to the Arts and Humanities Research Council for a Leadership Fellowship, which enabled me to complete this book. Many thanks to the Poetry Society for the 2017 Peggy Poole Award, to New Writing North for a Northern Writer's Award, to *Mslexia* magazine and Seren for their Women's Pamphlet Prize, and to Creative Futures for a Creative Futures Literary Award.

'Imagines' was commissioned by Carol Ann Duffy for *The Guardian Review*'s 'Into Thin Air' anthology, on declining insect populations. 'Muirburn' was commended in the 2017 National Poetry Competition. 'Kindling' won *Ambit*'s 2019 poetry competition, under a different title. I am thankful to the editors of the following magazines and anthologies for featuring poems from this book, some of which appeared in different forms: *anthropocene*, *Ambit*, *The Best New British and Irish Poets 2019-2021* (Eyewear Publishing, 2021), *The Forward Book of Poetry 2022*, *Magma*, *The Manchester Review*, *Mslexia*, *The North*, *The Poetry Review* and *Wild Court*. Many of these poems appeared in the pamphlets *Translating Mountains* (Seren, 2017) and *Spikenard* (smith | doorstop, Laureate's Choice, 2019). Part of 'Fossil Record' appeared in the pamphlet *Deerhart* (Knives, Forks and Spoons, 2016).

The Wordsworth Trust's mentoring scheme enabled me to work with Zaffar Kunial, whose generous advice has been instrumental in the creation of this book. I owe a great debt of gratitude to Pascale Petit, who helped me to shape this collection during the Jerwood-Arvon mentoring scheme. I am thankful to Deryn Rees-Jones, Ahren Warner, Grevel Lindop and Fiona Benson for their wisdom and encouragement.

A Hawthornden Fellowship and a residency sponsored by the Fondation Ledig-Rowohlt provided valuable time and space for me to complete many of these poems.

'In Oils' draws on testimonies and accounts of the first Gulf War, including the false 'Nayirah Testimony', Amnesty International's 'Iraq/Occupied Kuwait' report on human rights abuses (1990), the documentary *Fires of Kuwait* (1992), Salah

Nasrawi's coverage of Operation Desert Storm in Baghdad, and an interview in *The Atlantic* with the photographer Kenneth Jarecke. 'Fired Earth' was inspired by the work of potter Steve Harrison. 'Waterland' owes a debt of gratitude to a range of literary sources, including Steve Ely's *The European Eel*.

Many thanks to colleagues, and especially to Alan Rice and David Morley, for your encouragement and collegiality. Thanks also to the John Muir Trust for a travel grant and for featuring 'The Flower that Breaks Rocks' on their website.